Buckie
in old picture postcards volume 1

by Eric Simpson

European Library   ZALTBOMMEL/THE NETHERLANDS

The author:
Eric Simpson was born in Buckie and is a graduate of Aberdeen University. A former Head of History at Moray House College in Edinburgh, he has lived at Dalgety Bay in Fife since 1966. His other books include 'Discovering Banff, Moray & Nairn' (John Donald), 'The Vikings in Scotland', 'Dalgety – the story of a parish', and 'The Auld Grey Toun – Dunfermline in the time of Andrew Carnegie 1835-1919'. He is the author, too, of the following European Library publications – namely, 'Aberdour and Burntisland in old picture postcards', 'Inverkeithing and Dalgety in old picture postcards' (with George Hastie), 'Dunfermline and Rosyth in old picture postcards' (with George Robertson), and 'Cowdenbeath in old picture postcards' (with George Robertson).

Acknowledgements:
Many people have helped in one way or another, but special thanks are due to the following: Jean and Bill Hendry, Ian Strachan (Banff), Jenny T. Duncan, James Mackay, Ian Stephen, Brian Wilkinson, Alex Cowie (Cornal), A. Dallas, Jean Mackenzie and E. Simpson (Mosstodloch). I am grateful also to Peter Reid, Isobel Harrison and other members of Buckie District Fishing Heritage Society and also to Mike Seton, Tony McCreadie and other staff of Moray District's Department of Leisure and Libraries for their invaluable help and assistance. Thanks are also due to Moray District Libraries for permission to reproduce photographs 23, 56 and 57.
As ever, I am exceedingly indebted to my son Fraser for photographic assistance and to my wife Kathleen for her patience, proof-reading skills and other indispensable forms of support.
This book is dedicated to my sisters – Jenny, who now lives in Dumfries, and Russie, now sadly deceased.

Cover picture:
In this mid-1930s view of Cluny Square, Alexanders' bus office, with petrol pumps outside, is in the far corner next to Menzies, hairdresser's. To the right of Thomson's boatyard, we see Bage's fish-curing yard. The arched-roofed electric power station built in 1932 is on the left. Buckie Town Council ran its own electricity department, managed by Arthur Black. This building was later incorporated into the boatyard.

BACK IN TIME

GB ISBN 90 288 5933 0

© 1994 European Library – Zaltbommel/The Netherlands
          Eric Simpson

Third edition, 1998: reprint of the original edition of 1994.

INTRODUCTION

Commercial photographers always hone in on a few favoured locations and in Buckie these are Cluny Square and Cluny Harbour. Both are appropriate choices. The Square is the centre point of New Buckie, the late 18th century planned town founded by local laird Cosmo Gordon of Cluny; and the harbour, initiated by John Gordon of Cluny, has, since the first stages were completed in 1880, been recognised as one of the finest in the north of Scotland.

As its name implies, New Buckie was by no means the first settlement in the area. Present-day Buckie is an amalgam of villages each with a fairly long and distinctive history. Buckpool, or Nether Buckie as it used to be called, dates back, we are told, to 1645 and Easter Buckie to at least 1723. These settlements, and others nearby like Portgordon, Portessie, Findochty, Portknockie and Cullen, were developed by their lairds, who saw the rich fisheries of the Moray Firth as an economic resource worth exploiting. Portgordon, for instance, was created in 1797 by the 4th Duke of Gordon, who brought some fisher families from Buckie to help kickstart his new planned village. Over the years the fishermen of Buckie and district earned an enviable reputation for their daring and seafaring expertise. It was indeed the skill and enterprise of their fisher families that ensured that the coastal communities were able to thrive and prosper.

Skill was not enough by itself. Without good harbours, the fishermen would have moved elsewhere, especially when larger vessels became the norm with the 19th century growth of the herring industry. The construction of Buckpool harbour in 1857 saved Buckie from inevitable decline. Even then, it had its disadvantages and Buckpool was replaced as the major port of the area when the new, deepwater Cluny Harbour was completed. When steam drifters came into general use in the early 1900s, the Town Council purchased the harbour and commenced a series of improvements, extending the north breakwater and adding extra basins. This was the time when the fishermen of this area from Portgordon to Cullen invested heavily in the new steam drifters, which were all the more necessary as the herring had moved further away from the coast. The steam drifters' range, reliability and speed allowed the Buckie district fishermen to pursue the shoals of herring round the coast of Britain. Though the steam drifters were much more expensive than the Zulus and other sailing craft that they replaced, they were potentially far more profitable. Indeed the pre-1914 years were for Buckie and its satellite villages a golden age of growth and prosperity. And the symbol of prosperity for these seafaring communities was the herring steam drifter. In 1913 276 steam drifters were listed on the Buckie register (BCK). This was more than a third of the total Scottish fleet, a far higher proportion than any of the other Scottish ports.

It is perhaps appropriate that the town's new maritime heritage centre, opened in 1994, whose focus is the history of the herring industry, is entitled 'The Buckie Drifter'. The centre-piece in the display areas is a stunning dry land recreation of an old-time steam drifter.

Up to comparatively recent times, the wives and daughters of the fishermen played an indispensable role. 'No man can be a fisher and want a wife,' it was always said. In the auld days, the women worked like slaves. Their multifarious tasks included gathering and shelling mussels for bait, mending nets, baiting lines, gutting and smoking fish and trailing round the countryside to sell their 'caller herring' and other fish. In the heyday of the drift-net herring fisheries, the gutting quines, both young and old, followed their menfolk. Where the driftmen went, so did the fisher quines to toil for long hours gutting and packing herring on exposed and usually shelterless quays.

The prosperous years did not last. The post-1918 collapse of the herring trade affected Buckie very badly. When Peter Anson made a return visit to Buckie in 1934, he was dismayed to find 'almost the same atmosphere of hopeless despair that one finds in the depressed areas of South Wales or Durham'. In 1938, 900 Buckie fishermen were registered as unemployed. The population by then had declined, as unemployed fishermen and shore-workers sought employment elsewhere. Extension of the burgh boundaries (incorporating Gordonsburgh and Ianstown in 1901 and Portessie in 1903) and a booming economy had brought the population in 1911 to its peak at 8,897. According to the 1991 census, it now stands at 8,012.

The neighbouring towns and villages also began to decay, although in the case of Cullen its decline went further back. Its population had peaked in 1891, but then sank slowly for some decades and then more rapidly in the interwar years. The population in 1921 stood at 1,986, but ten years later it was down to 1,688. Far-seeing locals, recognising that Cullen was facing inevitable decline as a fishing port, sought to improve its image as a tourist resort. In Buckie, likewise, during the depression years of the 1930s the Town Council, seeking to attract more summer visitors, showed enterprise in expanding facilities for golf (at Strathlene and Buckpool) and developed Strathlene as a recreational area, providing, among other amenities, an open-air swimming pool.

The recovery in the fishing industry began in the 1950s, when the availability of government grants and loans meant that the fishermen of the Banffshire coast were able to invest in modern dual-purpose motor vessels. As before, the fishermen themselves owned most of the boats using the well-established share system. Modern, very expensive equipment was installed and new methods were introduced. With herring overfished, the fishcatchers now concentrated on white fish and Norway lobsters (for scampi). The revival of fish processing and other ancillary trades like boat-building helped the town towards a new period of prosperity. Today, though, the fishing communities again face an uncertain future. Consequently Buckie, which is too heavily dependent on a single industry, will have to undergo further adaptation. Whatever happens, the sea and seafaring activities will be vital factors in a town whose motto is an exceedingly apt one – MARE MATER, which means the Sea our Mother.

1. It was a long-standing complaint among the business community of Buckie that the burgh was off the beaten track and thus lost passing trade. The painted sign on the former Inchgower Inn was one solution to the problem. The inn was strategically placed next to the toll house, where once drivers of horse-drawn carts and carriages stopped to pay the tolls which were levied to meet maintenance costs on the main east-to-west turnpike road. These once prominent landmarks were demolished in the 1950s to improve sight lines for modern traffic.

218581.J.V.   HIGH STREET, BUCKIE.

2./3. Travellers coming down the High Street entered the New Town of Buckie. The Commercial Hotel on the left is marked on an Ordnance Survey map of 1870. These particular photographs date from (left) the early 1930s and (right) the late 1930s. In the later view we observe that there are petrol pumps at Webster's Garage (on the High Street since at least 1908). The new electric lampposts are also promi-

High Street, Buckie

nent as is the War Memorial, still in its original location. The shops include Nicol's, painter, Thomas Paterson's grocery and, opposite the latter, Charlie Milne's boot and repair business. The earlier photograph shows an auld street wallie (bottom left) and across the street an older style of lamppost.

High Street Buckie.

Valentine's Series

4. Victorian-age travellers could find 'good' accommodation at the Cluny Hotel (1880) on the Square on the right. Both the Cluny and the Commercial Hotels advertised their stabling and posting facilities. In this card, which was posted in Buckie in 1903, only horse-drawn vehicles are visible, so there is plenty of dung on the street. The shop fronts on the extreme left, John Green's and the Globe Market, are single-storied. By the time the next photograph was taken, the frontage had been raised another storey. (See also No. 7.)

Square and Established Church, Buckie

82110.

5. The pedestrians peching up the brae into Cluny Square didn't have a great deal of traffic to cope with. Contrast the grass-covered banks, which are left in 'a state of nature', with the steps, railings and terraces that were later added. (See the cover photograph.) The size of the Square indicates that the original planners doubtless hoped that New Buckie would become an important market centre like Keith or Elgin. Looking at the wide empty space available, we see also why many, but not all, saw this as the obvious location for the post-1918 War Memorial.

6./7. Quite a few of the citizens have been gathered for this circa 1900 set-piece photograph which we present here in two separate sections. Cycling had become popular judging by the number of bikes for sale and hire at George Webster's Cycle Depot (left). Women are evidently valued customers for the Hobart and Coventry Cross bicycles on sale here. One bike is still in its delivery crate. On sale at Alex.

Esson's drapery are boaters and other garments, and at Alexander Lyon's (right), which is very much a Johnny A-things type of store, we see a huge variety of hardware, ironmongery and other goods. Outside Lyon's there is an old-style lamppost and since it is summertime the glass has been removed. The hand-cart and the wheelbarrow outside would have been used for delivery purposes.

8. The high mortality rate during the Great War 1914-1918 left its mark on the community. Armistice Day commemorations in the 1920s brought large crowds to mourn the men who had sacrificed their lives in this fearful conflict. The crowd here is extra large as this was a special occasion, the unveiling and dedication of the Buckie War Memorial in 1925. There is still an ironmonger's shop in the Square, but the proprietors are now R. Tindall & Sons. Geordie Webster has gone from the Square and Alex. Esson has flitted into his former premises.

Buckie looking West from E. C. Spire.

2.18584 J.V.   EAST CHURCH STREET, BUCKIE.

9. In the top postcard, which was published by J.P. Pozzi, we see in the foreground two of this 'weel kirked' toon's places of worship. The Fisherman's Hall (1886) is the dominating feature in the Seaton. 'Pretty place up here; and nice boys!' wrote the sender when she posted the card to Glamis in June 1917. In the lower postcard, we note that the North of Scotland Bank (which was later absorbed by the Clydesdale) is now facing the Square and ornamental lamps also now flank the War Memorial.

BUCKIE. LOOKING EAST FROM E.C. SPIRE. 155 / 12

10. The straight lines of the planned New Town of Buckie show up clearly in this photograph. We see too how limited in size the town was. On what is now Cliff Terrace, the lighthouse is visible, but there are no dwellings to be seen and open fields surround the embankment of the Highland Railway line (top right). The Post Office also has still to be built. There is plenty of washing out to dry in the back yards, but the late 19th century residents of East Church Street couldn't complain of road traffic noise.

11. Looking now in the other direction along West Church Street, we note the railings fencing off the twa kirks. This card (postmark date 1905) demonstrates how rapid was the growth of the burgh in the last three decades of the 19th century. This thoroughfare was built up after East Church Street and, as late as 1870, while the road line was visible, there was not a single building on West Church Street.

EAST CHURCH STREET, BUCKIE.   Nº 12

12. This circa 1950s view shows how traffic on East Church Street had increased, but not enough to cause any parking problems nor pose much hazard for cyclists. Most shops then were privately owned, like on the right the Globe Stores, a grocery, and opposite the substantial premises of James Mackay, draper and ladies' and gents' outfitter. On the sunny south-facing side of the street the sun-blinds are down.

Cliff Terrace and Lighthouse, Buckie

13. Three young cyclists pose for the camera at the top of McLaren's Brae. This card, posted to Dayton in Ohio in November 1913, shows the 'new' houses in Cliff Terrace built in the burgh's Edwardian heyday. Many of these substantial dwellings were occupied by well-doing drifter skippers who had moved up the brae from the Seatown or Yardie. No. 4 is under construction. A decrepit hedge encloses the grassy area in front. Cluny Estate planted ornamental trees in this area, which was locally known as 'The Plantation'.

St. Peter's Road, Buckie

14. Heading west into Buckpool, we observe the handsome villas in St. Peter's Road that went up during the late 19th century expansion and which reflect, as with the dwellings in Cliff Terrace and elsewhere, the prosperity which resulted from the boom in the herring fishing industry. Notice in the top picture the lad atop the Edwardian-style lamppost and in the lower, late 1930s card the electric lamp attached to the telegraph pole.

Victoria Bridge & R. C. Church, Buckie.

15. A visitor wrote in 1905: 'This is the bridge which collapsed when almost finished...' This collapse had taken place four years earlier and was still obviously a talking point. Apart from the Victoria Bridge and St. Peter's Roman Catholic Church, we see some of the St. Andrew's Square buildings and part of the Roman Catholic school on the right. In 1891 the average attendance at St. Peter's School was 284. Again we see a lot of children posed for the photographer. In those days bairns could safely play tackie, kick-the-cannie, or hiplicks (hopscotch) in the streets.

West Church Street, Buckie

16./17. Although at first sight not much has altered in West Church Street between circa 1914 and the late 1930s, a closer look reveals changes in dress, street lighting and road surface. Notice in the right-hand picture fishermen's garb 1930s style. At the beginning of the century, Alexander Dallas sold groceries, ironmongery and china at his shop at the West Street/West Church Street corner. In the 1930s view, the proprietor at No. 68 was J.C. Munro. In the early years of the Second World War these premises were

218582.

WEST CHURCH STREET, BUCKIE.

utilised as the headquarters for the local, wartime Special Constables. Further on Eddie Hillocks' garage can be seen, just a short distance from Mrs. Campbell's sweetie shop. The railings on the right were removed for scrap to aid the war effort during the Second World War. What is now Cluny School then still had its spire.

WEST CHURCH STREET, BUCKIE.

218583.

18. This card posted in July 1937, shows that when the photograph was taken the film 'Tonight's The Night' was the 'big picture' at the Playhouse. James Archibald's 'Penny Palace' was purchased by Caledonian Associated Cinemas. After being refurbished in 1937, prices went up. In May 1939, adult prices at the Playhouse, 'the most modern and up-to-date Picture House, on the Moray Firth Coast', ranged from 6d to 1/6d. Next-door we see the Buttercup Dairy and across the street James Mair, butcher, and F.F. Angler, watchmaker and jeweller.

West Church Street, Buckie 9.

19. Further along West Church Street, we come on the left to the premises of G.P. Gibson, chemist and bookseller. He had 'all school books and requisites in stock.' Another speciality was his own hand-cream, Gibson's Ivy Balm. Next door there was a shoeshop, the Dundee Equitable. Mrs. Masson, across the road, sold tobacco, fancy goods and sweeties. Sutherland's shoeshop and Fowlers' bakery with attached 'Luncheon and Tea-room' were among the other long-established businesses nearby.

Buckie Seatown   *from Buckpool Harbour*

20. Going back in time, we see youngsters playing on the beach and old salts claikin at Buckpool Harbour. Most of the boats are Scaffies and there is not a steam boat to be seen. It was the building in 1857 of the harbour at Nether Buckie, as it was then, that laid the basis for the remarkable growth in the prosperity of Buckie and its fishing community. Behind lie the Yardie and the Seatown. Buckpool Harbour, which was always prone to silting, was filled in and landscaped in the late 1970s.

The Yardie, Buckie.

21. Around 1823 there were just three houses in the Yardie; the rest was cultivated ground, part of which was used for fishermen's yairds or allotments. In this early 20th century postcard we see the simple but and ben style of cottage that was characteristic of the early fisher touns. The original dwellings would all have been thatched. Note the gey roch looking roads and also the contrasting roof styles. Some dwellings that have been fitted with roof tiles have skylights, whereas those that are still thatched lack this amenity.

Mending the Nets

22. The house in the centre of the picture in this old view of the Seatown was one of several which had a thacket roof. Windows were small because glass was expensive. Nets and gear could be stored in tarry lean-to sheds or in special stores. Women's work was essential to the success of the fishing community. Here we have a group of women mending herring nets. As the next illustration shows, selling fish round the farms and landward villages and towns was another traditional aspect of women's work. Shawlies were, of course, popular garments.

23. The trains on the Heilan Line carried the older fishwives, like those shown here at the Buckie Highland Railway station, to Drybridge and other stations on the line to Keith. The Buckie Heilan Line station building at the back of Garden Lane was purchased by Buckie Town Council in 1939 and flitted to Strathlene, where it served as the clubhouse for Strathlene golf course until 1973. The Highland Railway branch line to Buckie and Portessie was opened in 1884. Most of the rails were lifted in 1915 for wartime needs and, though later replaced, the Heilan Line in effect was finished.

Baron Street, Buckie

RELIABLE SERIES 971

24. The distant buildings have been touched up in this early 1900s view of Baron Street. Notice the police uniforms of the day (right). A contemporary guide-book tells us that large herring boats were laid up on the beach over the winter. They were then launched for the summer season, leaving behind just a few old hulks. The rounded bows indicate that most of the boats visible here are of the Scaffie type. The straight stempost of BF 1220 indicates that this vessel must be either a Fifie or a Zulu. BCK registrations date from 1907.

Buckie from Seatown

25. We are still down in the Baron Street and Bank Street area. Baron Street was then an important thoroughfare. In this view we see now the sharply-raked stern of the by then obsolete Scaffies. The shed and fenced-in yard of George Thomson, boat-builder, where there is a boat on the stocks, also stand out. Buckie Gaslight Company's gasometers also feature in this card, which was published by J.P. Pozzi of Elgin and posted in July 1911.

Buckie Harbour

26./27. The early years of the 20th century saw the Buckie herring fleet transformed as the transition was made from sail to steam. It was not just the Scaffies but the newer Zulus, seen here in the left-hand postcard, that were now out of date. The Buckie district fishermen, to a greater extent than any others in Scotland, sold or scrapped their sailing craft, took out mortgages and bought the new faster and more powerful steam drifters. The 'Girl Lily' (BCK 115), whose crew are shown right, was built by Portgordon

boat-builder William Geddes. Notice, in the Edwardian-period postcard (left), what looks to be piles of stones on the quayside probably ballast from one of the boats that pack the harbour. There are some fine, strapping chiels among the fishermen. No females, though, are to be seen. In the old days, if any women were encountered when fishermen were heading to their boats prior to sailing, bad luck would ensue. It was also bad luck to take ballast from an old boat and put it in a new one.

49   **BUCKIE FROM HARBOUR**

28. Sailing craft did not disappear altogether. Unlike the vessels that were being used some fifty to sixty years earlier, these boats are decked. Although they are sailing boats, they also carry long oars or sweeps which were essential if the wind was to drop leaving boats becalmed. Lifeboatmen in those days had also to row their boats. The R.N.L.I. boathouse, built in 1884 for the lifeboat, can be seen centre-left and behind it the North of Scotland Bank's harbour branch. This bank played a key role in financing the purchase of gear and boats. Observe the small dwelling to the right of the Marine Hotel.

Buckie from the Harbour.

29. As now, Buckie harbour was used for commercial traffic. Colliers brought coal to the town. Salt for the fishcurers and timber were other important imports, and, of course, large quantities of herring were shipped to the Baltic countries. In the left-hand picture we see two of the larger sailing ships that were typical of the cargo boats that served the community, also a small fishing boat and a couple of Scaffies. Regrettably, the cupola of the old fishmarket building on the left is now removed.

30. Some of the local fleet of steam drifters are seen within the by now extended harbour (top picture). Their greater speed (10 to 11 knots) gave them the advantage over sailing craft when taking their catch back to harbour, and their longer range meant that fishermen were able to follow the shoals of herring right round the coast. Proud owners, doing well at, say, Yarmouth, commissioned oil paintings of their drifters. Here we see a 1911 painting of the 'Thrush', which was owned by James, Peter and George Cowie (Cornal), depicted near Smith's Knoll lightship.

The Harbour, Buckie

31. This postcard reveals the close ties between the fishing industry and the railway network. GNS on the waggons stands for Great North of Scotland Railway. Some waggons carry logs and others fish barrels. The card was posted in January 1913 by a seaman to his wife in Torry, to tell her that they are safe at Buckie although the weather had been awful. 'We have heard about the Brackenhill,' he continued, 'that is a bad job.' This reference is presumably to a maritime disaster.

Cluny Harbour from Parish Church Tower, Buckie

32. Steam drifters pack the harbour which had then only two basins. Nor had the breakwater been extended. The change from sail to steam as the primary means of propulsion was the great revolution that transformed the herring fishery in the early 1900s. By 1914 the Buckie district ports owned no fewer than 298 steam drifters. In 1908 Buckie Town Council purchased the harbour from Cluny Estate. Although the postmark of this card is August 1920, the photograph dates back to the early 1900s. The holiday maker who sent this postcard had enjoyed a lovely motor run and praised the good weather.

GALA DAY, BUCKIE HARBOUR

33. There are lots of spectators, including a solitary cloaked figure, to be seen in this Gala Day view. Buckie Swimming Club, founded in July 1901, held their galas in this basin. As with the photographs on the previous page, we note the absence of the lifeboat shed, which was not erected until 1922. The shed on the left, with the drain pipes stacked at the rear (far left), are plumbers' premises – proprietors J. & T. Campbell. In Martin's engineering works' yard (right) a traction engine, partly covered by a tarpaulin, can be seen. In the early 1980s the west basin was filled-in to provide cargo storage space.

Fish Market, Buckie, Harbour

C 626

34. In this between-the-wars postcard, the leading drifter is BCK 203, the 'Lea Rig'. Barrels are being unloaded from the horse-drawn lorry. All in all there are a lot of barrels piled up on the quay. The steam drifters of the Banffshire coastal communities were always freshly-painted and kept spick-and-span, even in the depths of depression. Superstitions regarding the presence of women have evidently been eroded. In 1953 the Buckie steam drifter fleet was reduced to two. By the following year there were none, diesel-engined seiners having replaced them.

35. This postcard published by Aberdeen photographer George Washington Wilson shows the railway station around 1900. The people waiting for the train coming from the Elgin direction are all wearing hats or caps. None has a suitcase, but there is a pile of trunks on the trolley. On the left we see the water-tower which was essential for providing water for the steam locomotives. The railway was closed in 1968 and the buildings demolished in 1980. The former R.N.L.I. boathouse can be seen top right.

Buckie from Portessie

36. The more substantial two-storey houses at Ianstown (formerly spelled as Eionstown) are in stark contrast to the older dwellings in the Yardie and Seatown. We see on the right houses with net lofts that were specially-designed and built for fishermen. The lofts have their own separate outside staircase. Additional storage space for herring nets and gear was essential, since the larger Zulus and the steam drifters were carrying many more nets. Notice, to the east of Cluny Harbour, the empty ground where Herd and Mackenzie later built their Buckie boatyard (see No. 60).

Peterhythe

Portessie

37. Where there was a hythe, a sheltered location where small fishing boats could be beached, fishing settlements were developed – as here at Peterhythe, Portessie. The large shed seen in this card (posted in 1907) belonged to William McIntosh, boat-builder. Founded around 1820, the Sloughy yard built over 900 boats. A son, William R. McIntosh, established another boat-building yard at Ianstown in 1893 and his boatshed is just visible (top right).

The Chapel

The Mause

Newton Brothers, Cullen, Buckie and Banff

Portessie, looking East

38. We observe a carefully-posed group of Sloughy loons in this Portessie view (postmark date, November 1908) and, on the foreshore, an array of drying poles and also some tarry sheds used for storing and barking (tanning) herring nets. The sender, a locum minister, has identified the building that was then the Methodist Chapel and also the Manse. His message reads: 'Our congregations are often small, as the men mostly are away fishing 9 months of the year – in the Yarmouth district just now.'

PROMENADE, PORTESSIE

39. A 1930s visitor described Portessie as 'the most higgledy-piggedly, picturesque village you ever saw'. What a difference, though, there is comparing this 1950s view with the previous picture. The promenade had been built, and the tarry sheds and drying poles had gone. A public lavatory (now removed) had been constructed. In the 1950s, too, Portessie could still boast its own railway station complete with a holiday camping coach. The Coast Line, however, closed in 1968.

V.A.D. Hospital and Kitchen, Portessie.

40. In January 1915, soon after the start of the Great War, the practically new hall of Rathven Parish Kirk was converted into a 26-bed VAD (Voluntary Aid Detachment) Hospital. The local Red Cross volunteers, with professional help from Dr. Duguid, looked after sick and wounded military personnel. The nearby cookery room of Portessie School served as both kitchen and canteen. The school cookery teacher and her pupils helped to prepare the meals. Bert, the sender of this card, remarked that it was not very big and that it was in a lonely spot but 'it is nice'. (See also No. 74.)

Strathlene, Portessie

41. This early 1900s postcard shows Strathlene House (which dates to 1887) when it was the residence of William G. Bryson, agent or factor for Seafield Estates. Thirty years later the house and grounds were acquired by Buckie Town Council and subsequently developed by the Council under Provost Merson as an amenity area. The purpose was to provide recreational facilities that would both be of benefit to the townsfolk and would also draw in visitors to help counterbalance the herring fishing industry that was by then in a state of catastrophic decline.

STRATHLENE HOUSE AND PUTTING GREEN, NEAR FINDOCHTY.

42. In this 1930s view, we see a Strathlene that has now been municipalised. There are a chain-link fence and a putting green, but the tearoom has still to be added. The house became a hotel, owned and administered by Buckie Town Council. A delighted guest wrote in 1953: 'An ideal spot to bring a family – sands, bathing, swimming pool, putting green, golf, all at the house.' (Regarding the golf club pavilion, see No. 23.) In 1984 Strathlene House was divided into four self-contained dwellings.

STRATHLENE AND PORTESSIE

43. By bus, car, bike and on foot crowds flocked to Strathlene. The sun-seeking trio seated beside the hotel – the year is 1948 – are the author's parents and elder sister. The tearoom behind them was a pre-war addition to the hotel. By the time the postcard (bottom) was despatched to Edinburgh in 1958, Strathlene tennis courts had gone and the area was serving as a car park. The salmon bothy – see drying poles, nets and coble on the beach – was, however, still a working enterprise.

44./45. By the 1930s healthy out-of-doors pursuits, like dookin and sunbathing, were all the rage. In 1932 Buckie Town Council constructed an open-air swimming pool at Strathlene with the stated aims of encouraging swimming and providing a tourist attraction. In 1934 the bathing pool was extended, with a sea-wall and extra changing rooms being welcome additions. During the 1930s swimming galas and

STRATHLENE POOL, BUCKIE

10

'aquatic sports' in aid of local charities were popular events. In the early 1950s, this writer had a holiday job as custodian of this unheated but highly popular facility. In those days the ticket office was just a tiny wooden cabin. The pond was filled by pumping in seawater when the tide was high. Sadly, this once highly-regarded amenity is now derelict. The left-side photo is mid-1930s; the other, judging by style of dress and cars, is late 1940s.

LINZEE GORDON PARK, BUCKIE

46. The Linzee Gordon Park, or Cluny Park to give it its old name, was another valued amenity and was used for a variety of leisure pursuits, although as the notice (right) states cycling was banned. Charles Arthur Linzee was the heir to the laird of Cluny. An ugly carbuncle of a building has replaced the original shelter-cum-toilet block shown here. The monument remains, but the attached drinking fountain has gone. The gates, manufactured by G.L. Smith & Co., Glasgow, are unchanged.

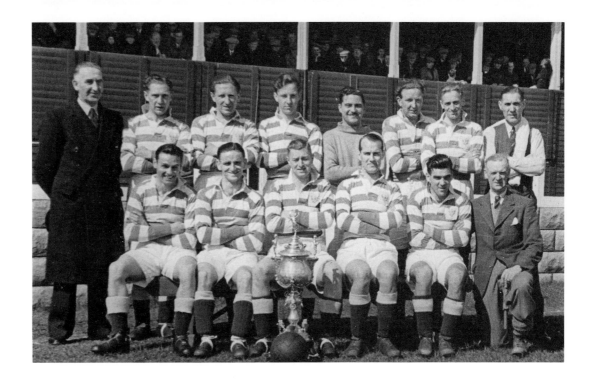

47. In 1946 Buckie Thistle won the Aberdeenshire Cup, their first post-war trophy. That same season the Jags also won the Aberdeen and District League championship. (The Highland League was not re-started till the following season.) Rome Tocher (manager) is on the left and the other backroom staff are pre-war stars, Abbie Gowie and Sandy Middleton. Like several others in the team, the captain, W. Brierly (front row, centre), was a serviceman stationed at one of the local air bases. The local players include Joe Hendry, Dod Johnston, Willie Laing and Faber Smith. Apart from the loonie in a balaclava, bunnets are the preferred headgear among the supporters.

Buckie.

Bowling Green and Tennis Court.

The Wrench Series, No. 20036

16/1/05

48. Posted in 1905, this card shows the recently-opened bowling green, which dates from 1901, and the tennis courts which were inaugurated in the following year. Up the brae L.T. McGarth took advantage of a prime site for advertising his ironmongery wares. The East Church Street skyline now looks very different. There was no Auld Kirk hall then.

Tennis Courts, Buckie

49. This postcard, which was also posted in 1905, shows the tennis courts and its pavilion from a different angle. Their coaties (sandshoes) aside, the tennis players have no special sports clothes and some even retain their hats and ties. Notice the partially-completed boat on the stocks at George Thomson's boatyard. The first steam drifter built at this yard was launched in 1903.

HIGH SCHOOL, BUCKIE

50. In the 1930s photo, loons are playing fitba on the open space where the Primary School was later built. When completed in 1926, the secondary department flitted from the West Church Street building, where the photograph of staff and senior pupils was taken in 1924-1925. The Rector, C.W. Thomson, is in the centre. He wrote 'Scottish School Humour' and was an avid pussyfoot (prohibitionist). Balfour Downie (1905) had the honour of being the first to have his name inscribed on the Dux Boards. The staff include Miss Lessels and Messrs. Coutts and Stephen, all well-known to successive generations of High School pupils.

51. The drill hall of Buckie High School, adorned with patriotic shields and sports trophies, is the setting for this set-piece photograph of the senior school orchestra. In 1939 gym slips were de rigeur for girls, and school ties are worn by girls and boys alike. Although some of the boys are wearing shorts, others have graduated to langers. Incidentally, the Dux medals that year went to Isobel F. Sandison and Ian T. Stephen.

"LADY CATHCART'S" SCHOOL, BUCKIE (NEW SCHOOL).

52. The Lady Cathcart School was founded by Mrs. Gordon of Cluny (later Gordon Cathcart) as a female industrial school. This episcopalian school could accommodate 150 bairns. It was the Toony School in popular parlance and was rebuilt in 1939. The building now houses a playgroup.

The Manse, Rathven

Rathven, Buckie

53. Judging by the size of Rathven Manse, clergymen enjoyed considerable status. Margaret, the sender of the top postcard, has marked the bedroom she occupies in the parish kirk manse. 'We are bathing and driving very often,' she wrote in July 1908. The kirk, which had been largely rebuilt in 1794, comes into the circa 1900 view of auld Rathven (lower postcard). Just to the left of the kirk, there is a corn-mill powered by water

Gollachy Mills Buckie.

54. Another water-mill features in this card (posted in 1907). We see in the foreground a mill dam with two sluice gates. The height at which the wooden lade enters the wheelhouse (i.e. the lean-to building on the right) indicates that the water-wheel must be of the overshot type. The 'Old Mill of Gollachy' is identified as a woollen mill on a map of 1870. In June 1893, we learn from a newspaper report, John Dawson's woollen mill at Gollachy was destroyed by fire.

Port Gordon from Station

55. Portgordon railway station on the Great North of Scotland's Coast Line was opened in 1886. In 1940 the suspicions of the railway staff here led to the apprehension by P.C. Bob Grieve and the author's father, Inspector John Simpson, of two German spies. They had arrived offshore in a German seaplane and had paddled ashore in a rubber dingy. A third spy who travelled south from Buckie station was arrested in Edinburgh. Now the rail track has been replaced by a coastal footpath and the station by a bowling green.

56. These waist-coated fishermen are sorting their nets at Portgordon harbour. Notice the cork floats on the nets on the right. In this Edwardian-period photograph, all three men and all the boys too are wearing bunnets or caps. Although the loons seem well enough dressed, all three are barefit. At least one of the fishermen is wearing leather seaboots. The three loons may well have gone to sea when they were old enough. In 1901 the male fishing population of Portgordon totalled 295 – including both men and boys.

57. Dressed in their Sunday braws and doubtless weel scrubbed, these gleeful Portgordon bairns head off for their Sunday School treat. Several are carrying their own mugs. On this occasion, all the loons, so far as we can see, are well-shod – stout boots with plenty of tackets on the soles being the favoured form of footwear. The harbour in the background was completed in 1874, but the harbour improvements at Buckie had a deleterious effect on Portgordon's trade.

GORDON STREET PORTGORDON

58. Like the Seafields in Cullen, the Dukes of Gordon are well-commemorated in the village of Portgordon. As with the other fishing communities of the Banffshire coast, the dwellings are attractively painted and well cared for. Notice the outside stairs leading to a net loft at the rear of the house on the right. Electric street lights are attached to the telegraph poles, so by this time the village's nickname of the 'Paraffin City' had ceased to be applicable. Up the brae to Crown Street (lower picture), we see Bill Bremner arriving with the milk delivery from Mill of Rathven farm. (See No. 53.)

Findochty

59. In this card of Finechty, which was posted in July 1903, the waggons and barrels on the boat shore indicate that some small-scale curing is being carried on. Once more we see fairly new two-storey dwellings with outside stairs leading to net lofts. In 1901 there were 119 fishing boats in Finechty and 330 fishermen and boys. But, as boats increased in size and the number of nets multiplied, so the disadvantages of the smaller harbours became more apparent. Most of the boats to be seen in Finechty nowadays are pleasure craft, moored at the marina within the harbour.

Findochty, New Town

60. This card (postmark date 1907) shows two steam drifters under construction at the Crooked Hythe, Findochty. It was the demand for steam drifters that brought James Herd and Thomas Mackenzie north to Banffshire. By August 1914, 32 drifters had been completed at the yard. Expansion in 1919 saw Herd and Mackenzie start building and repairing boats at Buckie as well as Finechty.

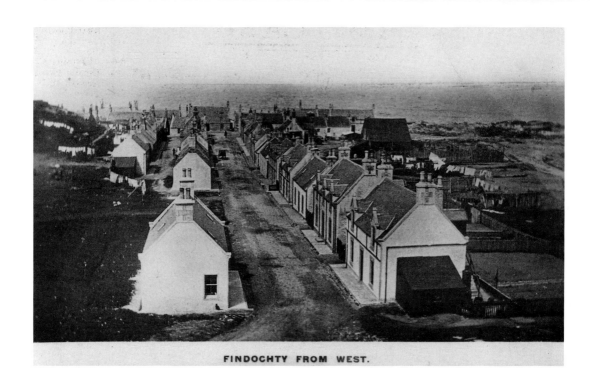

FINDOCHTY FROM WEST.

61. While Findochty from the West is the caption on the card, this photograph showing Duke Street and New Street was actually taken from the south-east. This community remained thirled to the fishing industry. In 1938 the Findochty fleet totalled 47 boats, 24 of them motor boats, the other 13 being steam drifters.

Newton Bros, Cullen, Buckie and Banff.

Portknockie.

Banffshire

62. In the 1880s and 1890s the Banffshire fishermen favoured the Zulu type of craft in preference to the Scaffie. The fleet of Zulus drawn up on the shore and the piles of barrels piled up ready for the fish curers show what a busy place Portknockie was. This photograph emphasises the cliff-top nature of this settlement and the extra work involved in removing the catch and taking gear to and from the boats. But, as the next photograph emphasises, the hythe (or sheltered cove) was a natural harbour which, especially when piers were added, gave very good protection.

Port Knockie Harbour

63. The harbour piers at Portknockie were constructed in the late 1880s. In this view we see no steam drifters, only sailing boats. There is a smiddy on the left and a number of curing yards which gave seasonal employment to the local fisher quines. When this card was posted in August 1913, Portknockie's population was around the 1,700 mark. Writing in 1928, Peter Anson described the fishers of Portknockie as up-to-date and go-ahead compared to Cullen. The burgh's 58 drifters employed 555 fishermen

Baiting the Lines, Portknockie

64. Some of Portknockie's 'go-ahead' fishermen were photographed while shallin mussels (left) and baiting the lines. Notice too in this set-piece photograph the fish hanging up to dry, also the finely-crafted baskets and sculls. No plastic or metal containers then. The Knockers, like fishermen elsewhere, favoured bunnets and gansies (guernsies), often with their galluses on top of the gansy.

"Reddin' the Lines," Cullen

65. Here we have another group of fishers, but this time at Cullen and, though both cards are undated, this one is probably further back in time. Putting bait onto hooks and, as here, reddin (i.e. unravelling) the lines were always attractive subjects for photographers. Picturesque though these scenes were to visitors, hand-line fishing, nevertheless, was labour-intensive and very hard work for men and women alike. In the background we see painted canvas buoys hung up to dry. Many years earlier, inflated pigs' bladders and dogs' skins were used to support nets in the water.

Newton Bros, Cullen, Buckie and Banff.

Seatown Cullen.

66. Although the storage buildings in the foreground were originally part of a farm steading, the Seatown was mainly inhabited by fisherfolk. In 1901 Cullen possessed 79 boats and 249 fishermen and boys earning their livelihood from the sea. The fishing boats at that time as seen here were a mixture of Zulus and Scaffies. The large lug sails are hoisted, possibly to dry them. Landmen, like the coopers who made barrels and the carter, with his cart full of barrels, at the bottom of the picture, got a lot of trade from the fishing community.

EBBTIDE. CULLEN BAY.

67. Some of the boats seen in the last photograph were doubtless built in the large shed which formed part of Gardiner's boatyard, which lay to the east of Cullen harbour. In 1907 twenty men were employed at the yard. This large arch-roofed shed remained in use as the business continued on a small scale until the 1940s. The shed was destroyed by a gale in 1953. The long low walls to the left are the ruined remains of Falconer's rope walk. Roperies were another of the important ancillary industries that helped to sustain the old fishing communities.

CULLEN BAY & SCARNOSE.

LORD & LADY SEAFIELD AT CULLEN HOUSE.

68. This 1920s Seatown view shows the contrast between the more upmarket two-storey dwellings on Castle Terrace and the older but and ben cottages behind them. We note too the Temple (left), a 19th century folly, the golf clubhouse and the 1884 railway viaduct, which had to be built only because the Seafield family had insisted that the railway be kept well away from Cullen House. The influence of the big hoose was omnipresent in Cullen. Here we see the new Earl and Countess of Seafield being ceremoniously welcomed as they take up residence in Cullen House in July 1912.

CL 8   THE SQUARE, CULLEN   A TUCK CARD

69. The Square symbolises the straight lines and formal layout of New Cullen – the Earl of Seafield's 19th-century planned new town. In this late 1940s view, the Town Hall is still in a ruinous condition after a destructive fire in 1942. The Seafield Hotel (right) could then boast that there were hot and cold water basins in all bedrooms. We observe to the left of the bus stop queue a Lipton's van and a car with a rear window blind. Regretfully the old-style traditional, red telephone kiosk has now gone.

Castle Street, Cullen

73889 (JV)

70./71. North Castle Street, as photographed in Edwardian days, provides an interesting contrast to the Seafield Street of the early 1950s. Compare the forms of street lighting, road surface and building styles. Observe the street wallie near the foot of Castle Street. By the mid-20th century street water pumps were redundant. Instead, though, we note the presence of petrol pumps in Seafield Street – Shell on the

59018   SEAFIELD STREET, CULLEN.

left and Esso on the right. Services were then still being held in the former Seafield United Free kirk, on the right side of Seafield Street, but since the union of 1929 the congregation had come under the auspices of the Church of Scotland. Today this elegant Gothic revival kirk houses 'Allie's Saleroom'. While the minister cared for the spiritual needs of the congregation, the policeman, in the police station next door, kept a watchful eye on potential malefactors.

THE THREE KINGS. CULLEN

AT THE SANDS, CULLEN.

72. With the harbour and fishing in decline, the folk of Cullen capitalised on their other assets, the foremost being the splendid beach and links. Facilities were thus provided for golfers and bathers. However, around 1900 gowffers (top postcard) wore every day clothes, including collars and ties. The huts to the left of the Three Kings rocks were built as changing-rooms for dookers. Note the voluminous bathing costumes drying on the line. In the bottom card (posted in 1926) we see costumes that are becoming less restrictive. But most of the bairns are wearing protective sunhats.

GOLF CLUB HOUSE AND SANDS, CULLEN.

Photo: Balfour, Cullen
Copyright

73. Cullen, locally proclaimed as 'the Brighton of the North', appealed to holiday-makers who sought a quiet holiday away from the crowds. But, aware of the need to keep up-to-date, the Town Council built the additional bathing huts that we see along the shore. To ensure too that the gowffers had decent facilities, the Burgh Council had this imposing clubhouse erected in 1930. It replaced the old clubhouse that we noted in No. 68. Judging by the vehicles on show, the photograph was taken in or around 1937.

RED CROSS HOSPITAL. CULLEN.

74. Like Buckie with its VAD Hospital at Portessie (No. 40), Cullen had its own temporary hospital during the 1914-1918 war. Donated by Seafield Estates factor James Campbell as a 'respite centre', it was manned by Red Cross volunteers. Today 'Campbell House' is divided into flats. The convalescent soldier who sent this card in September 1916 to his parents in Kentish Town, London, was glad that they had dodged the Zeppelins. But the parting injunction from this hard-up Tommy was: 'Hurry up with that money.'

75. When war threatened once again at the time of the Munich Crisis in 1938, local naval reservists were mobilised. Here they are seen en route to Buckie railway station. War, averted on that occasion by the Munich Pact, broke out in the following year. Thus evacuees from Edinburgh arrived at the railway station in Buckie in September 1939. Here we see some evacuees, with Police Sergeant John Simpson keeping a wary eye on the proceedings, being packed into the lorry that was to transport them to their new temporary abodes.

76. Concluding with a peacetime parade, we return to the High Street, where the Ist Pack of Buckie Brownies is heading for the South Kirk. The date is June 1957 and the Brownies are parading to mark Empire Youth Sunday. Like the British Empire, premises like Jannetta's ice cream parlour, Easiephit, Lipton's grocery and Sutherland's furniture shop have departed from the scene. Gone too are all-British car marques like the Austin on the far right. Flitted too from its old central location is the War Memorial, built to commemorate those 'heroes of the Empire' who sacrificed their lives in 'the war to end all wars'.